Updat Gout CookBook Series (Snacks)

Discover A New 20+ Gout friendly Snacks For Reversing And Healing Gouty Arthritis

Mary J. Hart

Table of Content

Cubes of Watermelon

Ingredients :
- 1 little watermelon

Instructions :
1. The watermelon should be washed in running water.
2. Slice the watermelon down the middle longwise.
3. Take one portion of the watermelon and put it cut-side down on a cutting board.
4. Cut the watermelon's rind off with a sharp knife, following the shape of the fruit.
5. Cut the flesh of the watermelon into cubes of the desired size after removing the rind.
6. With the remaining watermelon half, carry out the procedure once more.

7. Put the cubes of watermelon in a bowl or other airtight container.
8. Whenever wanted, refrigerate the watermelon 3D squares for an invigorating and chilled nibble.
9. Serve the watermelon 3D shapes with no guarantees or enhancement with a twig of new mint for added newness and show.
10. Partake in the succulent and hydrating watermelon 3D shapes!
11. Planning time: 10-15 minutes

Greek Yogurt Parfait with Fresh Berries and Almonds

Ingredients:
- 1 cup Greek yogurt,
- 1/2 cup fresh mixed berries (strawberries, blueberries, and raspberries, for example),
- 2 tablespoons chopped almonds,
- 1 tablespoon honey (optional)

Instructions :
1. Layer half of the Greek yogurt at the bottom of a glass or bowl.
2. Add a layer of blended berries on top of the yogurt.
3. Over the berries, scatter a tablespoon of chopped almonds.
4. With the remaining Greek yogurt, berries, and almonds, continue layering.
5. If you want the top layer to be sweeter, drizzle honey over it (optional).

6. Decorate with a couple of entire berries and almonds on the top.
7. Serve right away and partake in this scrumptious and protein-rich Greek yogurt parfait!
8. Preparation time: Healthy snack for 5 to 10 minutes

Guacamole with Carrot Sticks

Instructions :

- 2 ripe avocados, diced,
- 1 small tomato,
- 1/4 cup finely chopped red onion, minced garlic, and
- 1 tablespoon freshly squeezed lime juice.
- salt and pepper to taste.
- 1 carrot sticks.

Instructions :

1. The avocados should be cut in half, the pits removed, and the flesh scooped into a mixing bowl.
2. Using a fork, mash the avocado until it reaches the desired consistency.
3. To the mashed avocado, add the diced tomato, chopped red onion, minced garlic, and lime juice. Combine thoroughly.

4. You can season the guacamole with salt and pepper to your liking. If necessary, adjust the seasonings or lime juice.
5. To prevent the guacamole from browning, cover the bowl with plastic wrap and place in the refrigerator for at least 30 minutes to allow the flavors to combine.
6. Give the guacamole a quick stir before serving. Taste and change the flavoring if vital.
7. Plan carrot sticks by washing and cutting carrots into long, slim strips.
8. Arrange the carrot sticks alongside the guacamole in a serving bowl.
9. For a tasty and healthy snack, serve the guacamole with carrot sticks.
10. Preparation time: 10-15 minutes (barring refrigeration time)

Quinoa Salad with Cucumber

Ingredients:

- 1 cup cooked quinoa
- 1/2 English cucumber, diced
- 1/4 cup slashed new mint leaves
- 2 tablespoons newly crushed lemon juice
- 1 tablespoon extra-virgin olive oil
- Salt and pepper to taste

Instructions :

1. Cook quinoa as indicated by bundle guidelines and let it cool totally.
2. Combine the chopped mint leaves, diced cucumber, and cooked quinoa in a mixing bowl.
3. In a different little bowl, whisk together the lemon juice, olive oil, salt, and pepper to make the dressing.
4. Pour the dressing over the quinoa combination and throw delicately to

equitably cover every one of the fixings.

5. If necessary, taste and adjust the seasoning.
6. To allow the flavors to combine, wrap the bowl in plastic wrap and place it in the refrigerator for at least 30 minutes.
7. Give the quinoa salad a quick stir before serving.
8. Place the quinoa salad in individual bowls or a serving dish.
9. Alternatively, you can decorate with extra new mint leaves.
10. Enjoy this quinoa salad, which is both refreshing and full of nutrients, chilled.
11. Planning time: 20 to 25 minutes (without refrigeration)

Smoked Salmon Cucumber Nibbles

Ingredients :
- 1 English cucumber
- 4 ounces smoked salmon
- 2 tablespoons cream cheddar
- New dill for embellish

Instructions :

1. Cut the cucumber into rounds that are about 1/2 inch thick and thicker.
2. Place the cucumber slices on a flat platter or plate for serving.
3. Each cucumber slice should have a thin layer of cream cheese on top.
4. Place the rolls or small pieces of smoked salmon on top of the cream cheese.

5. A small sprig of fresh dill should be added to each cucumber bite as a garnish.

6. Enjoy these elegant and delicious smoked salmon cucumber bites right away!

7. Planning time: 10 minutes

Feta and Roasted Red Pepper Dip

Ingredients:

- 2 cooked red peppers (from a container or newly simmered)
- 1/2 cup disintegrated feta cheddar
- 2 tablespoons extra-virgin olive oil
- 1 clove garlic, minced
- 1 tablespoon lemon juice
- 1/4 teaspoon dried oregano
- Salt and pepper to taste
- New parsley for decorate

Instructions :

1. The roasted red peppers should be drained, patted dry, and then roughly chopped.

2. In a food processor or blender, join the slashed red peppers, disintegrated feta cheddar, minced garlic, lemon juice, dried oregano, salt, and pepper.

3. Mix the fixings until smooth and all around consolidated. If the dip is too thick, thin it out by adding a little olive oil or a tablespoon of water.

4. If necessary, adjust the seasoning by tasting the dip.

5. Move the plunge to a serving bowl and sprinkle with extra-virgin olive oil.

6. Use fresh parsley as a garnish.

7. With whole-grain crackers, pita bread, or vegetable crudités, the roasted red pepper and feta dip is a great accompaniment.

8. As a gout-friendly snack, enjoy this flavorful and creamy dip!

9. Planning time: Healthy snack for 15 minutes:

10.

Roasted Spiced Nuts

Ingredients

1. 1 cup mixed raw nuts (almonds, walnuts, cashews, and pecans, among others)
2. 1 tablespoon melted coconut oil
3. 1 tablespoon maple syrup
4. 1/2 teaspoon ground cinnamon 1/4 teaspoon ground cayenne pepper (optional, adjust according to taste)
5. 1/4 teaspoon salt

Instructions:

1. Your oven should be preheated to 350°F (175°C).
2. Salt, melted coconut oil, maple syrup, ground cinnamon, and ground cayenne pepper (if using) should all be

combined in a bowl. Mix thoroughly to combine.

3. Add the blended crude nuts to the bowl and throw them with the flavored combination until equitably covered.

4. On a parchment-lined baking sheet, arrange the coated nuts in a single layer.

5. Broil the nuts in the preheated stove for around 10-15 minutes, or until they become brilliant brown and fragrant. Mix them more than once during baking to guarantee in any event, toasting.

6. Allow the nuts to cool completely after taking them out of the oven.

7. Transfer the spiced roasted nuts to a serving bowl or airtight container once they have cooled.

8. Serve the nuts as a gout-friendly snack that is crunchy and delicious.

9. Planning time: 20 to 25 minutes

wholesome snack for Tuna and Cucumber Roll-Ups:

Ingredients:

- 1 enormous cucumber
- 1 can (5 ounces) fish, depleted
- 2 tablespoons plain Greek yogurt
- 1 tablespoon slashed new dill
- 1 tablespoon lemon juice
- Salt and pepper to taste
- Toothpicks

Directions:

1. Using a mandoline slicer or a vegetable peeler, slice the cucumber lengthwise into thin, long strips.

2. Add the drained tuna, plain Greek yogurt, chopped fresh dill, lemon

juice, salt, and pepper to a mixing bowl. Combine thoroughly.

3. Spread out a cucumber strip on a spotless surface and spot a spoonful of the fish combination toward one side.

4. Secure the end of the cucumber strip with a toothpick as you gently roll it up tightly.

5. Rehash the cycle with the leftover cucumber strips and fish blend.

6. On a platter for serving, arrange the cucumber and tuna roll-ups.

7. Serve immediately or chill until serving time.

8. Partake in these reviving and protein-rich cucumber and fish roll-ups!

9. Planning time: 15-20 minutes

Zucchini Chips Baked

Ingredients:

- 2 medium zucchini,
- 2 tablespoons grated Parmesan cheese,
- 1/4 teaspoon paprika,
- 1/4 teaspoon garlic powder,
- salt and pepper to taste,
- cooking spray, or olive oil

Instructions :

- Pre-heat the oven to 425°F (212°C). Use olive oil or cooking spray to lightly grease a baking sheet or line it with parchment paper.
- Wash the zucchini and cut it into 1/8-inch-thick thin rounds. Wipe

them off with a paper towel to eliminate overabundance dampness.

- Combine the salt, pepper, garlic powder, paprika, and grated Parmesan cheese in a small bowl.

- On the baking sheet that has been prepared, arrange the zucchini slices in a single layer.

- Spray the zucchini slices lightly with cooking spray or drizzle olive oil over them.

- The Parmesan cheese mixture should be evenly distributed over the zucchini slices.

- The zucchini chips should be baked for about 15-20 minutes, or until they are crispy and golden brown. To keep them from burning, keep a close eye on them.

- Once prepared, eliminate the zucchini chips from the stove and let them cool for a couple of moments.
- Place the baked zucchini chips on a plate or bowl for serving.
- Partake in these delightful and virtuous heated zucchini chips as a gout-accommodating tidbit!
- Planning time: 25-30 minutes

Chickpea Salad with Spices

Ingredients :

- 1 can (15 ounces) chickpeas, washed and depleted
- 1/2 cup diced cucumber
- 1/2 cup diced tomato
- 1/4 cup cleaved new parsley
- 2 tablespoons cleaved new mint
- 2 tablespoons finely cleaved red onion
- 2 tablespoons newly pressed lemon juice
- 2 tablespoons extra-virgin olive oil
- Salt and pepper to taste

Directions:

1. In a blending bowl, join the washed and depleted chickpeas, diced cucumber, diced tomato, cleaved

parsley, hacked mint, and finely slashed red onion.

2. To make the dressing, combine the olive oil, salt, and pepper in a separate small bowl.

3. Toss the chickpea mixture with the dressing to ensure that it is evenly coated.

4. If necessary, taste and adjust the seasoning.

5. Cover the bowl with saran wrap and refrigerate for somewhere around 30 minutes to permit the flavors to merge together.

6. Prior to serving, give the chickpea salad a speedy mix.

7. Place the chickpea salad in individual bowls or a serving dish.

8. Serve chilled and partake in this reviving and protein-pressed chickpea salad.

Chickpea Salad with Spices

Ingredients :

- 1 can (15 ounces) chickpeas, washed and depleted
- 1/2 cup diced cucumber
- 1/2 cup diced tomato
- 1/4 cup cleaved new parsley
- 2 tablespoons cleaved new mint
- 2 tablespoons finely cleaved red onion
- 2 tablespoons newly pressed lemon juice
- 2 tablespoons extra-virgin olive oil
- Salt and pepper to taste

Directions:

1. In a blending bowl, join the washed and depleted chickpeas, diced cucumber, diced tomato, cleaved

parsley, hacked mint, and finely slashed red onion.

2. To make the dressing, combine the olive oil, salt, and pepper in a separate small bowl.

3. Toss the chickpea mixture with the dressing to ensure that it is evenly coated.

4. If necessary, taste and adjust the seasoning.

5. To allow the flavors to combine, wrap the bowl in plastic wrap and place it in the refrigerator for at least 30 minutes.

6. Prior to serving, give the chickpea salad a speedy mix.

7. Place the chickpea salad in individual bowls or a serving dish.

8. Serve chilled and partake in this reviving and protein-pressed chickpea salad.

9. Planning time: 15 minutes (barring refrigeration

Grilled Pineapple with Chili Lime

Ingredients:

- 1 ready pineapple
- 1 teaspoon bean stew powder
- 1/2 teaspoon lime zing
- 1/2 teaspoon ground cumin
- Spot of salt
- New lime wedges for serving (discretionary)

Instructions :

1. Adjust the heat to medium on a grill or grill pan.
2. Slice the pineapple into rounds or spears about 1/2 inch thick after peeling it.

3. In a little bowl, join the bean stew powder, lime zing, ground cumin, and salt to make the flavoring.

4. Press the seasoning mixture into the flesh of the pineapple by evenly spreading it out on both sides.

5. Place the seasoned pineapple slices on the grill or grill pan that has been preheated.

6. The pineapple should be grilled for about two to three minutes on each side, or until it has slight caramelization and grill marks.

7. The grilled pineapple should be taken off the heat and allowed to cool for a few minutes.

8. The grilled pineapple can be served as is or with fresh lime juice added for extra citrus flavor (optional).

9. A delicious snack that is good for gout is this grilled pineapple, which is tangy and slightly spicy.

10. Planning time: For 10 to 15 minutes,

Greek Yogurt Fruit Parfait

Ingredients:

- 1 cup plain Greek yogurt
- 1 tablespoon honey or maple syrup
- 1 teaspoon vanilla extract
- 1/2 cup mixed berries (blueberries, strawberries, raspberries, etc.)
- 2 tablespoons chopped nuts (almonds, walnuts, etc.)
- 1 tablespoon unsweetened shredded coconut (optional)

Instructions:

1. In a little bowl, combine as one the plain Greek yogurt, honey or maple syrup, and vanilla concentrate until very much joined.
2. Select a glass or container for layering the parfait.

3. First, spread a layer of Greek yogurt on the glass's bottom.

4. Add some of the mixed berries to the yogurt layer.

5. Sprinkle a tablespoon of hacked nuts over the berries.

6. Yogurt, berries, and nuts are added in a second layer to complete the layering process.

7. Shredded unsweetened coconut can be added as a final layer if desired.

8. If you want to make more parfaits, you can do the layering process again.

9. Serve immediately or chill until serving time.

10. As a healthy snack or dessert, this fruity, creamy Greek yogurt parfait is good for gout!

11. Planning time: 5-10 minutes

Toast with Sweet Potatoes

Ingredients:

- 1 large sweet potato Your choice of toppings (for example) avocado slices, cherry tomatoes,
- feta cheese, and fresh herbs) Olive oil Season with
- salt and pepper to your liking

Instructions:

- Your oven should be preheated to 200°C (400°F).
- Wash the yam completely and cut it longwise into 1/4-inch thick cuts.
- Place the slices of sweet potato on a parchment-lined baking sheet.
- Sprinkle olive oil over the yam cuts, then, at that point, season them with salt and pepper to taste.

- In a preheated oven, bake the sweet potato slices for 20 to 25 minutes, or until they are tender and lightly browned.
- Eliminate the yam cuts from the stove and let them cool marginally.
- Each sweet potato slice should be topped with whatever you like, such as avocado slices, cherry tomatoes, feta cheese, and fresh herbs, once it has cooled.
- The sweet potato toasts make a tasty and healthy snack that is good for gout.
- Planning time: 30-35 minutes

Cucumber and Greek Yogurt Plunge

Instructions :

- 1 English cucumber
- 1 cup plain Greek yogurt
- 2 cloves garlic, minced
- 1 tablespoon newly crushed lemon juice
- 1 tablespoon slashed new dill
- Salt and pepper to taste

Guidelines:

1. Grind the English cucumber utilizing a case grater or food processor.
2. Squeeze the excess moisture out of the grated cucumber with a clean kitchen towel or cheesecloth.

3. The strained cucumber, plain Greek yogurt, minced garlic, lemon juice, chopped fresh dill, salt, and pepper should all be combined in a bowl.

4. Combine all of the ingredients thoroughly with a fork.

5. Taste the plunge and change the flavoring as per your inclination.

6. Place the cucumber and Greek yogurt dip in a bowl for serving.

7. Sprinkle some fresh dill on top as an optional garnish.

8. Sliced vegetables like carrots, bell peppers, or cucumber rounds can be paired with the dip.

9. As a gout-friendly snack, enjoy this protein-rich, energizing dip!

10. Planning time: For 10 to 15 minutes,

Quinoa Stuffed Bell Peppers

Ingredients:

- 4 bell peppers, any color;
- 1 cup cooked quinoa;
- 1/2 cup diced tomatoes;
- 1/2 cup cooked black beans;
- 1/4 cup diced red onion;
- 1/4 cup chopped fresh cilantro; lime juice;
- ground cumin;
- chili powder;
- salt and pepper to taste sour cream, avocado slices, and shredded cheese

Instructions :

1. Set the oven temperature to 375°F (190°C).

2. Remove the highest points of the ringer peppers and eliminate the seeds and layers from within.

3. Cooked quinoa, diced tomatoes, cooked black beans, diced red onion, chopped cilantro, lime juice, ground cumin, chili powder, salt, and pepper are all included in a mixing bowl. Combine all of the ingredients thoroughly.

4. Spoon the quinoa blend into the emptied out chime peppers, pressing it in solidly.

5. Place the stuffed ringer peppers in a baking dish and cover it with foil.

6. The bell peppers should be baked for about 25 to 30 minutes, or until they are tender.

7. To allow the tops to slightly brown, remove the foil and continue baking for an additional 5 minutes.

8. Once cooked, eliminate the stuffed chime peppers from the broiler and let them cool for a couple of moments.

9. The quinoa-stuffed bell peppers can be served plain or with optional toppings like sour cream, avocado slices, or shredded cheese.

10. Partake in these delightful and nutritious quinoa stuffed chime peppers as a gout-accommodating tidbit or quick bite!

11. Planning time: 40 to 45 minutes

Roasted Cauliflower Bitelets

Ingredients:

- One medium head of cauliflower, two tablespoons of olive oil,
- one teaspoon of paprika,
- one teaspoon of garlic powder,
- one teaspoon of onion powder,
- one teaspoon of cayenne pepper (optional, adjust to taste), salt and pepper to taste, and fresh parsley for garnish.

Instructions :

1. Pre-heat the oven to 425°F (212°C). Use olive oil or parchment paper to lightly grease a baking sheet.
2. Cut the cauliflower into scaled down florets, disposing of the intense stem.

3. In an enormous blending bowl, consolidate the olive oil, paprika, garlic powder, onion powder, cayenne pepper (if utilizing), salt, and pepper. Mix well to make a marinade with flavor.

4. Toss the cauliflower florets gently in the marinade after adding them to the bowl until they are evenly coated.

5. Organize the cauliflower florets in a solitary layer on the pre-arranged baking sheet.

6. The cauliflower should be roasted in a preheated oven for about 20 to 25 minutes, or until they are tender and golden brown. Flip them partially through cooking for searing.

7. After the cauliflower bites have been roasted, take them out of the oven and let them cool for a few minutes.

8. Move the simmered cauliflower chomps to a serving dish and enhancement with new parsley.

9. Serve the roasted cauliflower bites as a gout-friendly snack that is both delicious and nutritious.

10. Planning time: 35 to 30 minutes

Greek Yogurt with Fresh Berries

Ingredients:

- 1 cup Greek yogurt
- 1/2 cup new blended berries (like strawberries, blueberries, raspberries)

Ingredients :

1. Begin by washing the new berries completely and wipe them off.
2. In a bowl or serving dish, spoon the Greek yogurt.
3. Put the new blended berries on top of the yogurt.
4. You can either blend the berries into the yogurt or leave them on top for an engaging show.
5. Serve right away, and enjoy!

Cucumber Slices with Hummus

Instructions:

- 1 large cucumber
- 1/2 cup hummus

Instructions :

1. Cut the ends off the cucumber after washing it.

2. Cucumber should be sliced into thin rounds.

3. On a plate, arrange the cucumber slices.

4. Place a dollop of hummus on each slice of cucumber.

5. For added flavor, you can sprinkle some spices or herbs on top as an option.

6. Serve right away, and enjoy!

Boiling Eggs

Instructions:

1. Over high heat, fill a saucepan with enough water to cover the eggs.

2. Add the eggs to the pan with care, and then bring the water to a boil.

3. When the water arrives at a bubble, decrease the intensity to medium-low and let the eggs stew for around 9-12 minutes, contingent upon your ideal degree of doneness (9 minutes for delicate bubbled, 12 minutes for hard-bubbled).

4. Prepare a bowl of ice-cold water while the eggs are simmering.

5. When the eggs are cooked as you would prefer, utilize an opened spoon to move them to the bowl of ice water.

Allow them to cool down and stop cooking for a few minutes.

6. Peel the shell off the eggs by gently tapping them on a hard surface to crack the shell.

7. Wash the stripped eggs to eliminate any excess shell sections.

8. Depending on your preference, you can either cut the boiled eggs in half or leave them whole.

9. The boiled eggs can be served plain or with additional seasonings like salt and pepper.

10. Boiled eggs are full of protein and delicious!

11. Planning time: Healthy snack for 15-20 minutes:

Almond Butter Celery Sticks

Ingredients:

- 4-5 celery stems
- 1/4 cup almond margarine

Instructions :

- Wash the celery stems completely and cut them into sensible lengths, roughly 4-5 inches each.
- Using a paper towel, dry the celery sticks.
- Spread almond margarine along the middle notch of every celery stick, filling it from one finish to another.
- On the other hand, you can likewise fill a little plunging bowl with almond spread and serve the celery sticks close by it.

- Organize the celery sticks on a plate or serving plate.
- Enjoy the crunchy and healthy combination of celery and almond butter right away!
- Planning time: Gout-Friendly Snack for 5 minutes:

Mozzarella-and Cherry Tomatoes

Instructions:

- 1 cup cherry tomatoes,
- 4-5 small bocconcini-sized balls of fresh mozzarella cheese,
- fresh basil leaves, and
- balsamic glaze (optional).

Instructions:

1. The cherry tomatoes have been washed and patted dry.

2. Depending on their size, divide the mozzarella cheese balls into quarters or halves.

3. Take a toothpick or little stick and string a cherry tomato, trailed by a piece of mozzarella cheddar, and a

new basil leaf. This should be done for the remaining cheese and tomatoes.

4. Organize the tomato, mozzarella, and basil sticks on a plate.

5. If you like, drizzle the skewers with balsamic glaze for extra flavor (optional).

6. Enjoy the delicious combination of sweet cherry tomatoes, creamy mozzarella, and fragrant basil as soon as possible.

7. Preparation time: 10 minutes -

Baking Kale Chips

Ingredients:

- Kale, one bunch, o
- ne tablespoon olive oil, salt, and pepper to taste

Instructions:

1. Your oven should be preheated to 350°F (175°C).

2. Use a kitchen towel or paper towels to completely dry the kale leaves after they have been thoroughly washed.

3. Tear the kale leaves into bite-sized pieces after removing the tough stems.

4. Drizzle olive oil over the torn kale leaves that are in a large bowl. To evenly coat the leaves with oil, gently toss them.

5. You can season the kale leaves with salt and pepper to your liking.

6. On a parchment-lined baking sheet, arrange the seasoned kale leaves in a single layer.

7. The kale should be baked for about 10 to 15 minutes in a preheated oven, or until the leaves are crispy and slightly golden. To keep them from burning, keep a close eye on them.

8. The kale chips should cool for a few minutes after being removed from the oven.

9. Place the kale chips on a serving plate or bowl.

10. Serve right away and partake in these fresh and nutritious heated kale chips!

11. Planning time: 20 to 25 minutes -

Cooked Chickpeas

Instructions :

- 1 can (15 ounces) of drained and rinsed chickpeas (also known as garbanzo beans)
- 1 tablespoon olive oil
- 1 teaspoon smoked paprika
- 1 teaspoon cumin
- 1 teaspoon garlic powder Salt to taste

Instructions:

1. Your oven should be preheated to 200°C (400°F).

2. Channel and wash the chickpeas completely, then, at that point, wipe them off utilizing a kitchen towel or paper towels.

3. Toss the chickpeas in olive oil in a bowl until well coated.

4. In a different little bowl, join the smoked paprika, cumin, garlic powder, and salt.

5. Sprinkle the zest combination over the chickpeas, throwing them tenderly to guarantee even dispersion of the flavors.

6. On a baking sheet that has been lined with parchment paper, arrange the seasoned chickpeas in a single layer.

7. Cook the chickpeas in the preheated broiler for around 25-30 minutes, or until they become fresh and brilliant brown. To prevent sticking, shake or stir the pan occasionally during cooking.

8. After the chickpeas have been roasted, take them out of the oven and let them cool for a few minutes.

9. Serve the roasted chickpeas in a bowl as a protein-packed, crunchy snack.
10. Planning time: 35-40 minutes

Almonds

Instructions :

- 1 cup crude almonds

Instructions :

1. Preheat your stove to 350°F (175°C) assuming you like to broil the almonds, or skirt this step on the off chance that you like to appreciate them crude.

2. On the off chance that cooking, spread the crude almonds in a solitary layer on a baking sheet.

3. The almonds should be roasted in a preheated oven for about 10 to 15 minutes, or until they are fragrant and slightly golden. To keep them from burning, keep a close eye on them.

4. In the case of appreciating them crude, avoid the broiling step and continue to the subsequent stage.

5. Allow the almonds to cool completely after taking them out of the oven.

6. Once cooled, move the almonds to an impenetrable holder or capacity sack.

7. Now is the time to enjoy them as a healthy and filling snack. You can likewise add them to trail blend or integrate them into different recipes.

8. Planning time: Gout-Friendly Snack: 15-20 minutes (for roasting) or no additional time (for raw almonds).

Printed in Great Britain
by Amazon

37583044R00036